Here
and
There

BRENDAN MULCAHY

THE CHOIR PRESS

First published in the United Kingdom in 2021 by
The Choir Press

978-1-78963-196-8

Here
and
There

for Catherine

Acknowledgements

Thanks to my wife, Catherine – life-force and daily *inspiratrice.*

Thanks to Jane and Rose for your sympathetic and insightful pre-readings.

Thanks to Miles, Rachel and Adrian at The Choir Press for clear advice and support at every stage in the production of the book.

Thanks to Kieran McCarthy for the cover photograph of Youghal Station. http://www.kieranmccarthy.com/

Thanks to Finnbarr Webster for the photograph accompanying *Boot Boy* on page 57 – finnbarrwebster.com

Cover photograph of mv *Innisfallen* courtesy of Corkcam.com

Photograph of 10 Downing Street, 24th July 2019 – WPA Pool, Getty Images

Representation of cover of *Richard II* – Penguin Random House

The epigraph is taken from Seamus Heaney's *The Spirit Level* (Faber and Faber)

In the poem *Well, Michelangelo Finished his Pietà at 24*, quotations from these two songs are acknowledged:

1   Wide Open Spaces by Susan Gibson (Bandcamp)

    … wide open spaces / room to make her big mistakes

2   Mr Rock and Roll by Amy Macdonald (Vertigo)

    I wish I knew you before.

You are neither here nor there,

A hurry through which known and strange things pass.

Seamus Heaney

Contents

i

ii

iii

iv

v

(i)

Flockdown

Wimbledon, Summer 2020

Pigeons populate

the 8 mm regulation lawns

at the AELTC.*

Over the road

geese gravitate

to golf club greens,

filling up

on fairways,

receding to roost.

Mowing and manicuring

go on,

golfers and croquet crew

poised

for the return

of their normality.

---

* All England Lawn Tennis and Croquet Club

What Will Survive?

for Maggie and Gareth

All week they'd raced at Cheltenham,
defying the odds: hands shaken and sanitised,
crowds sardined, winning connections
bear-hugged like there was no tomorrow,
until Al Boum Photo won a historic repeat Gold Cup.
No snaps record we met for lunch next day in Oxfordshire.
By Monday – with magnolia everywhere out – the fear was in.

For once we'd sailed through East Sheen. Held up at Kew,
the motorways were easy then, kites hovering,
before the B4009 through Watlington.
One ask – a man, a boy, a dog, when we'd
guessed wrong at an unmarked junction –
and we turned right, effortlessly on time
into The Chequers at Berrick Salome.

Brakspear! with its funky missing 'e's – implying
timelessness and ale from a well-kept cellar.
The tennis-club lot were in for a swift half,
red-faced and elbowing, owning the bar.
But we were up for it, teasing stories
from the Guardian and the *i*: times were
changing, ineluctably.

Then you were there, somehow without satnav help.
We fist-bumped good-humouredly for hugs,
and Maggie dear, ensconcing by the fire,
you murdered a large Merlot in a trice. We rued
the loss of the Six Nations, Gareth – though, truth to tell,
you'd most miss London Welsh at Old Deer Park.
Postponed? Cancelled? Fixtures were falling away.

We would have weighed the impact of the virus –
the *panic early, beat the rush* brigade
were stripping shelves in Epsom, as stunned
oldsters gaped. But it was a joyful meeting,
as though we knew something very good was ending.
Leaving, groups were gathered in the garden.
An unhurried kite circled overhead.

20th March 2020

The Arrival of the World King at No. 10

Downing Street, 24th July 2019

Under a Georgian fanlight,
on no red carpet but a wet-feet mat,
the world king lays claim to his realm.

For once his tie sits tightly on his collar.
For once his peroxide mop is groomed.
The suit's a step-up on his trademark shamble chic
but looks new on: it's not Macron.

Mouth taut; worryingly close-set eyes
avoid the camera; hulking, no-neck,
as though he's been photo-shopped porn-style.

Off-balance, the Cabinet Secretary – smile, Mark! –
has his hand crushed in a prime ministerial mangle.

A well-fed flunky orchestrates
the wan below-stairs underlings' applause.
They swell the progress, careful not to over-step the mark.
Still, a single office flip-flop shows.

Unnoticed, out of focus, eccentric,
Mephistopheles Dom lurks with his infernal machine,
a bishop's glide away down a Vermeer chess-board,
owning the show in Primark vest and trackies.

Love and Loss (i)

Half-term, Buckfast Abbey

Through Dartmoor rain my daughter runs
splattering up to the abbey's solemn doors.
Rebuffed, stands shivering, while her grandparents
negotiate the last stretch at a steady pace.
Her bobble hat has blown back from her face,
and shows the high brow her mother shares.
The scarf, that any moment now she'll lose
forever, wraps in coloured coils around her neck.
For a photographic second she's transfixed –
arrived, becalmed, wanting to know what's next,
so intense you'd swear there was a worry in her head.
I catch the moment that she tugs the scarf, and, out of shot,
my parents find sanctuary in the porch.

Love and Loss (ii)

You'd bought me, as a Valentine's gift,
a choice of Thomas Hardy's poems
and asked me to read one in bed.

I remembered Under the Waterfall –
There lies intact that chalice of ours –
from teaching Emma poems to the Sixth.

My glasses had been lost somewhere downtown –
the ones with the electric blue frames.
I sensed I'd get them back.

I began, *Whenever I plunge* –
eyes straining to decode
the ten-point font – *my arm, like this ...*

It was deliberate, arrhythmic stuff
and I foundered on *a fugitive day.*
You were laughing and told me to stop.

Jammed darkly, the dropped lovers' glass
had opalized beneath the waterfall.
In an internet café, in clear-eyed morning,
I knew I would retrieve my blue aberrant specs.

Gilt by Association

i
Golden glitter streams pre-play
on the beautiful boy prince.
Anointment, sceptre and orb,
Edward's crown, polyphony
conjure the new King Richard
in dumb-show before our eyes.

ii
Eden, demi-paradise,
begets Bushy, Bagot, Green,
commonwealth caterpillars.
Gaunt, expiring, chides the king.
England's landlord, ha! So much
for that. Now, for our Irish wars.

iii
Down, down I come like glistering
Phaethon, fluxed Icarus, to
the base court where kings grow base;
blushing, discontented, king
of misrule; unthresholded,
screaming Bacon hysteric.

iv
Wanamaker's wooden O
sees the hollow crown change hands,
roan Barbary usurped. So,
inoffensive shadows dance
the illusory away
and us out into the night.

v
Going home glittered on the tube,
quasi party animal.
Waking to pillow glitter
unexplained, with you in France.
Magicked when it dawns on me,
the fact of it, life gilded.

David Gentleman's
New Penguin Shakespeare *Richard II*

My New Penguin Shakespeare *Richard II*
says Bradford '81, with 30p in pencil.
Second-hand from somewhere – who knows where?
When was I ever in Bradford? Maybe twice.
The cover design – unmistakably David Gentleman – shows
Barkloughly Castle – *it doth contain a king* –
blocky, shadowed, all-encompassing.
Bolingbroke the usurper, furred and hatted
like a Cossack, floats mid-stage. His herald
hoists a partisan twice human height
towards a tower upper right,
where the king awaits
discoronation, absurd in scarlet daubs.

Quality Street

Under cover of darkness,
Henry moves among his *ruin'd* troops,
quells fears, stirs fight; it's Agincourt
and the odds are agin.
An extraordinary commoner bestows
a little touch of Harry in the night.

In the Alexandrian court, Antony
proposes to Cleopatra
that they *wander through the streets
and note the qualities of people.*
From Rome, austere Octavius sees them
*reel the streets at noon and stand the buffet
with knaves that smell of sweat.*

Centuries off, a critic calls out such
indecorous and degrading conduct,
slumming on the Arab street;
equates qualities with
quirks, misses
the implicit riches
the soldier general seeks.

How to intermingle
the purple and the people?
The largesse universal flows one way.
To talk with crowds and keep your virtue
presupposes proletarian vice.

Your Move

Mentioned in passing, as Octavius' shadow
takes the shine off Antony's forum coup,
Lepidus is just there,

agreeing without demur
his brother too must die.
Styled *a slight, unmeritable man,*
meet to be sent on errands.

Octavius and Antony spar, while
studious Agrippa primes the hoop.
Out of the loop, Lepidus buffers
and blesses futile nuptials.

On Pompey's barge Octavius forbears,
companionable Antony makes hay;
befuddled, butt of reptile jokes,
Lepidus, is borne away.

Denied rivality by Octavius, he's trashed.
Fool Lepidus! Antony fumes,
shackled perforce to his Egyptian dish,
his useful stooge removed.

The servants see it all: a triumvir
called into a huge sphere,
and not seen to move in't.

(ii)

Kettled at Millwall

We came in unmolested on the tube
to Bermondsey, lunched on Jamaica Road,
then walked down past Peek Frean towards the Den.
We'd read the runes: no divulging colours showed.

All unnervingly unremarkable,
passing for normal till it all kicks off –
like Clapham by day when bullets flew by night.
How would I get you out if push came to shove?

It was a draw, inconsequential stuff.
We'll take the point. Time we skedaddled.
You were cold and, as we say, delighted enough.
Next thing the Met moved in and we were kettled.

Encaged in metalled alleys, for our own good, we
    processed
like circus tigers, seemingly under arrest.

The South Africans Upstairs

The South Africans upstairs seemed fine,
her name Italian and he a Brett,
or a Brent – one of those.
Genial when we met them in the pub,
though she was quicker to break contact off.

When mice appeared, they left the key
so I could chaperone the rodent man.
Their life was orderly, they kept the kitchen clean,
and arranged their recycling exquisitely.

The Saturday they were three hours
in the Odeon watching Transformers
planted seeds of doubt.
Sheepishly, they agreed
it had not been time well spent.

On summer nights they migrated to their balcony.
It wasn't Durban, but, you know.
And so they stayed in every way discreet
but for the cannabis clouds cascading in on the wind.

Distinguishing Mark

Mark on his own, in his good overcoat,
hair neatly parted and oiled, Doc Martens trim,
watching his Doughboys struggle at the Dog and Duck,
down on the flood-plain of the Nene,
Tesco as yet unbuilt.

Half-time and he annotates *Lord Jim*
this time; he's fine with Beckett too.
Inclines to *Punctured bicycle*
on a hillside desoláte on the PA,
it being 1983.

Tried Birmingham once –
university … English … David Lodge –
but foundered on those east-west trains.
Was talked home from Kidderminster,
that box ticked.

On his fork-lift truck up at Kraft's,
mouth set, Mark sees all.
Kafka pokes
past the logo
on his mint corporate overalls.

O'Shaughnessy on his Bicycle

O'Shaughnessy goes riding
dead centre down the hill.
It's wide and cars are scarce, so
he'll stay out there until
he gets a premonition.
Oh yes, he's there until ...

Freewheeling like Free Willy –
the wind bags out his coats –
wilful as a stallion
out for its morning oats,
he rides, he rides, he's riding
like a stallion out for oats.

The chapel never sees him
in all things he is free,
undaunted by the lamp-post,
unthreatened by the tree,
and wholly undiminished by
the sky above the tree.

A catapult might take him out,
deployed with perfect aim,
but to smite him riding in his pomp
would be a perfect shame.
A choir of saints unbidden cries,
To kill him, it's a shame.

Banstead Bungalow Fish Pie Incident

There'd been a murder in the one at the corner,
years back, Jessie from next door confided.
A fourteen-bungalow close,
handy for Waitrose,
sixteen miles out,
and short on kids.

Trish and Brian came to stay overnight –
off somewhere in France again –
she invariably good news, he to be borne.

They lodged him with the cricket in the lounge
and set about fish pie for tea.
The necessary choppings and scrapings
and pre- this and that got done.
The pie was stowed.
Sauvignon and conversation flowed.

Lobster-faced, in time, the cricket over,
their neglected third party reappeared.

Where was the pie?

The pie was in the oven. Why the apoplexy?

Well, Michelangelo Finished his Pietà at 24

Sandwiched between Ordinary Elephant and The Plucking
    Idiots,
in the Red Dragon Listening Room in Baton Rouge,
the Susan Gibson – 5000 views –
holds court in Walmart comfort work jeans,
tells how, at forestry school in Missoula, Montana, she wrote
Wide Open Spaces and, unbeknowing, launched The Dixie
    Chicks.
Manhandles her dreadnought guitar but just can't reach the
    A on *of stone.*
A road warrior, in her forties now, still the ingénue
but the smart one-liners keep coming as she gamely
    celebrates
the Grammys, the world tours and sleek, blonde Sony
    success
of those girls, who also nicked a name from Little Feat.

      Wide open spaces

            room to make her big mistakes

Her greatest hit, her one-hit wonder, royalty pension,
CMA record of the year, one-off arrow to the heart of the
    bull,
and goose-bump, a cappella high school graduation gold.
At 19!

Lunching between Sainsbury's and the audiologist,
    at the Prince of Wales, on Broadway,
I'm ear-struck, held, by a song I can't really place but know I
    know.
Everyday extraordinary, cheap tune with the pints and the
    chilli,
but not banal; changing the day's deal, thrilling enough to
    make me
grab a pen and grab a line, *I wish I knew you before.*

Wingin' it, with a jumbo guitar,
at a Glasgow warehouse window, kohl-eyed Amy
belts out her anthem of foredoomed youth,
struggling with the E minor 7,
before plucking a happy ending from the air.
10 million views and loved in the threads –
On a scale of 1-10 it's 45!
I listen to this song every day. It makes me so sad.

Unrepeatable gold at just 19.
A decade on, turned blonde, with Greatest Hits,
she's married an ex-Rangers right back
who one time made the Scotland squad for the Slovenia
    friendly.

Public Relations

David Aaronovitch? No.
The suit is pressed, the beard kempt.
Even so, you have a clue:
the bulk, teased hair, suede shoes
of this figure who lingers,
rapt, on Waterloo concourse

at half-three on a Friday
afternoon. One o'clock strivers
walk clean lines; by five they dodge
and swerve to get somewhere.
But he's constrained, rocks
unconvincingly, but stays,

eyes fastened on a woman (*stage left*)
who negotiates a barrier
unsurely. Her ticket fails.
Neat hair mussed, she glances
back but does not re-engage,
drawn to other urgencies.

Forty playing fifty plus, she's
immaculate in black. They
could be in communications:
partners on projects, heads-ups,
break-outs, power-point pitches,
keeping channels open.

Casual Friday protocols
decree a bistro lunch.
Did he prefer veal schnitzel
beurre noisette, with Puligny-
Montrachet and she concur?
In just such ways, *les jeux sont faits.*

Out of tricks – he's overplayed his hand –
he reddens, half-smirks, vacillates.
She recovers, moves through
and in and on. Emptying,
he watches her away. A busker strums
Waterloo sunset's fine.

Unspeakable

Yeah, still CDs in this car, I'm afraid.
Looks like Miles Davis, Planxty, Lutosławski …
You pays your money and you takes your choice.

That crossed 'l' is a 'w', by the way, the 'w' a 'v'.
Oh, and the 'o's a schwa.
It's the *Best of Lutosławski* – Naxos, natch,
so you could be on a winner.
I recommend the fourth of the Jeux vénitiens,
where he began introducing randomness
into exact synchronisation. Just listen for the drums.
But they'll come for you in any case.

Bodhráns of plenty! Planxty, go raibh maith agat!
And sláinte mhaith, Turlough Ó Carolan,
Sightless visionary, bearer of the harp,
begetter of the uillean pipes of Flynn.

The Miles Davis is *Kind of Blue* …
Beyond reproach until *#MeToo*.

Whadda y' do?

The Rivals

Rival 1570s, from Latin *rivalis* "a rival, adversary in love, neighbour"; originally, "of the same brook," from *rivus* "brook"; "one in pursuit of the same object as another, or neighbourly competitor" – "one who uses the same stream."

Two rogues converged in a mellow wood
where a tree had fallen cross a stream,
allowing one to pass, while his opponent stood
to nod and wave, knowing well they could
not both traverse the trunk at the same time.

Robin, the younger, in Lincoln green, could see
at once he was expected to give in,
but was not minded to, and up spoke he.
Good fellow, pray you wait awhile for me.
These were brave words for young Robin.

His rival, a man gargantuan,
laughed loud and mock-applauded him.
Such arrogance in one only half-grown.
Like David with his catapult and stone.
Set one foot on that bridge and you'll be in!

He pointed. Notwithstanding, Robin took
a step the insubstantial crossing-place upon.
A thwacking stave the reckless upstart struck,
and flung him headlong down into the brook.

But unintended consequences happen, and, anon,
the enterprising outlaw had recruited Little John.

(iii)

———

Here and There

Our ship awaits below
And we must go.
All else ends here.

From now on we shall speak of there.

Summerhill, Summer 1959

Painting the Paddy sign,
Brendan Farrelly's dad
sways on his cradle,
high above Minto's Alsatians.

We're on the North side now,
in Granny's house, overlooking
the docks and the station
and the stables of the drays.

The money's all gone but the view is stellar.

Mr Mullaney lodges, toasting
his feet on the fender, nodding off.
He's a commercial traveller,
gives me sixpence to sort his work-sheets.

Millstreet, Mitchelstown, Macroom,
Mallow, Fermoy and Kanturk:
his life a North Cork odyssey,
a William Trevor Book of Days.

Me, Jesus?

Brendan, would you be Jesus today?
Sister Maria had sheltered me since
the Innisfallen crossing and the boat train
translated me to my North London primary.
Now she'd thrown me to the dogs.
I'd had my hand up to be picked,
secure in the knowledge that I wouldn't be.
We had sung in class at St. Patrick's in Cork
but classroom drama was a thing unknown.
I couldn't move or speak or think.
Encouraging cries of 'Go on. You can do it!'
fell on deaf ears. I froze.
No attempt was made to unfreeze me.
Stefan, would you …? And in seconds
qualm-free, streamlined Stefan was up on the desk
dispensing loaves and fishes
to a grateful multitude.

Lurking behind the blackboard some weeks on,
my motivation found, in a non-speaking role,
I helped to mug the Good Samaritan.

Fred Reeve in Excelsis

I look at some kids and they head the ball with the top of the head. Their technique is all wrong, so the pressure that it's putting on the brain is a lot more.

Ryan Mason, ex-Tottenham Hotspur, forced to retire early by a serious head injury.

Head it! the cry rings out.
The dark sphere descends
near where I'm planted,
astutely, you might think,
to receive the corner delivery.
Never having learnt to time the spring
that precipitates the ball towards the goal,
I stay ground bound.
Still, honour-bound to have a go,
latter-day Tom Brown, I watch it down.
The twain converge, the ball goes up not on,
and I'm left stunned, see stars –
shuddering, juddering to the margins
unattended.
Blackened brown and water-logged,
the sewn leather ball was lead, a shot-put
doinging on my head. It wouldn't happen twice.

Divert your gaze to fearless Freddie Reeve.
Not tall, but solid, comfy in his skin.
You could tell at a glance he'd climb and swim.
Wore his floppy platinum mop

fashionably long, though much
too much himself to strike a pose.
See him goofing, fringe in his eyes –
a Jubbly fills his face. Easy, fun,
a magnet for the girls from Sacred Heart,
all taken in his stride.
The school's left-half from the first pickings,
he kept his place unchallenged till the Fifth –
the Sixth Form was a step too far for Fred.
But he could meet a corner like a god.
His wherewithal, his lack of worry, equipoise
were not the stuff of coaching manuals.
He soared, made contact clean,
unfailingly compelled the orb
through rusting posts.

The Maths Problem

First week in grammar school, all new,
discovered HCF and LCM.
The lovely world of numbers now a code,
with worse to come, and worse – the maths problem.

I never lost a wink of sleep at sums
or doing calculations in my head.
Arithmetic had clicked. But now that easy pride
transmogrified into a dismal dread.

Shaven-headed, in his wheelchair, the Doc
took my certitude and sent me down a set
to a zone where cosines and calculus
distilled dissatisfaction and regret,

abolishing my shining morning face,
ineptitude and panic in its place.

We Called her Eaglebird

Uncle Michael's wife was Eaglebird.
They lived up the Met line from us in
Swiss Cottage, maybe Finchley Road.
We never met.

Black sheep Michael had led Dad astray,
the story went: the suitcase
that got nicked at Paddington;
the saved-up eighty quid they blew on drink;
the shiftless exile in a crumby flat.
The link was cauterized and life went on.

Back from university one time
I was taken to meet him at his bed-side.
He was still a handsome rogue
and told me I was too.
Hard to believe he'd be gone in a week.
I took to Ingeborg and never saw her again.

Stephen Louvain

In memoriam Stephen Louvain Mulcahy (1915-1994)

You were inordinately proud
of that exotic middle name, Louvain.
The third of four Stephens, men of Cork.

You never sought out Leuven (or *Louvain*),
burnt to hell the summer of '14,
the year before your blue eyes
first took in the River Lee.
The name sufficed,
your signature assertively S.L.

You followed the beaten path
to 50s London, rented a three-bed flat,
commuted every day from Harrow Met.
Irrevocably, the die was set.

You liked a pint and half-one, sure,
but most you craved the company
of those like you who read.
Your priceless gift to me every weekend
the Observer and (pre-Murdoch) Sunday Times.
You weren't drawn up the tribal Harrow Road
but, reared on Ring,
you went to Highbury for Haverty
and Twickenham for O'Reilly running
rings round hapless toffs in lily-white.

Fate would not contrive to bring you home
to spend your autumn days beside the Lee.
A wild goose separated from the skein,
a proud Corkonian, you remain
immortally, Stephen Louvain.

Making the Cut

Tom Sullivan, with his grooved face
and oiled grey hair,
fixed dilapidated shoes
in democratic piles;
done ones parcelled, stapled, labelled,
filed in individual cubby-holes.

Pared-down blades sent off-cuts
flying across the floor,
while you shone pennies
shiny on the buffer –
latent with unspoken grasp.

A lived-in, leather-smelling space
where an Irish wife
found solace and repair,
uprooted and unsure
in Middlesex mid-life.
Tethered to a clever man
who turned things over
but could not cut through.

(iv)

Providence

Would you mind if we sang for you?
Suzi and I have a routine to this song we like.
I'm leaving Providence, heading for the bus station.
Been staying on the west side, Federal Hill:
Italian, crime-ridden – watch yourself.
But my white-painted boutique hotel had been fine
and I got to visit Brown and, in a hippie shop,
was gifted a coloured glass ring,
which broke next day in the shower.
The roads are not easy to walk
so I break the journey for an unwonted Starbucks
and have the day's epiphany with the girls,
who sing karaoke and dance in their uniforms
without affectation, and with unalloyed provincial sweetness.

Clamming up

The Falmouth Quarterdeck. Summer. Cape Cod.
I write at one of those blessèd horse-shoe bars
where conversation sparks as naturally
as blonde tip-hungry barmaids importune.
The lady to my right asks what I write –
I show her my holiday journal.
She's seventy. Ann Fay. Perfection in her way,
but muscling in.
I should have seen it coming
but I'm stuck for an answer
when she says, 'You can help me finish these clams –
'He's got terminal cancer.'
On cue, he nods.

How we Spent August 2013

We called the printer Seamus after Heaney
died in August of that year.
One out, one in. So it goes. We'd been in
New York City, bought *Human Chain*
in the Strand Bookstore on Broadway
(a cheapskate black-spot copy – shame!)
returning to learn of our loss.

And in the Cube, the Apple Store on 5th,
we took the plunge and bought a MacBook Air:
a thousand bucks and more, an unexpected
spend, but proven justified, seven years on
now, with OS Catalina doing the job,
hand in hand with Seamus,
to produce poems.

Georgia on my Mind

On a wound-down, dressing-gown Sunday morning,
I hear Alistair Cooke's *Letter from America.*
His vowels bespeak an age gone by.

He's 88. His *playmates are all gone.* He's too unwell
to fly again to Georgia from New York,
where Tiger Woods, incipient ace at 22,
will win the U.S. Masters by 12 strokes.
Pre-Wiki, I take an atlas, trace the route.

Absurdly, now, in zero point five nine seconds,
with twenty million pages offered,
I know where,
how big, how far,
the gas cost – *50 bucks.*

Later in the Sunday churn,
I turn to Matthew Sweeney's *A Dream of Maps.*
By chance a traveller, off to the golf,
interrogates a Georgia gazetteer.
Alpharetta … Athens … Atlanta …
Augusta! Ball in hole!

Of all the poems in all the tomes on all the shelves …

New Jersey State of Mind

Our mission here at DMCNJ:
to create intuitive simplicity
by leveraging technological solutions
through a human-centric approach.

It's New Jersey, so it's faintly risible –
Richard Ford. Blow-in from Biloxi
but you know what he means.
(Did Governor Christie really block that bridge?)

Self-styled university mouse at Princeton,
Ford drove the Garden State Parkway
on a Jersey Shore reconnaissance,
as Springsteen, Freehold homeboy,
tallied silly New York virgins by the score
in Asbury Park and down on Bradley Beach,
loving and leaving Sandy, 4th July ...

then engineered that devastating break –
I was not my father's favorite citizen –
and it was independence day all down the line.
That father-son thing; fathers and sons.

Cue Frank Bascombe,
incubated by this time,
realtor of Haddam and Sea-Clift,
in Ford's own New Jersey state of mind.
One son lost, he'd take his other boy
to Cooperstown in *Independence Day*,
to save him at the Baseball Hall of Fame.

As if.

Cool Kid on the 4 Train

You in blue
and your peanuts dip-
                    able.
You're cool.
You eat-em-when-u-wan-em.

Mom's red matches your belt.
She's leaning out and
                    down,
gripping,
gripped by
one fat, bent-
        back paperback,
absorbed behind monster specs.

You're attuned to the rhythms of each other.
You're attuned to the rhythms of the 4 train.
You're attuned to the rhythms of the world.

Anyone seen Mac?

The farm was long gone.
McDonald, older, shifted west
(pulling the plug on all that quack-quackery and E I O)
to an Alaskan infinity
of polar bears, Palins and salient aliens.
Had a farm. Had to fly.
He don't have to justify.

(v)

Wine and Water

Panem et circenses – bread and circuses (Juvenal)

Tap water works to mitigate the wine
on tables now,
in restaurants, at parties, or
just staying home hydrated while a match
plays or a film runs
alongside some Rioja or Cab Sauv.

Learning the rules of booze at sixth form dos,
nights of Double Diamond and Red Barrel
left you felled, furry-mouthed, forlorn;
paralytic in a Sunday morning agon
a pint or two of water would assuage.

So why not now have water, leave the wine?
The cost alone – say ten cases a year –
That's twelve and a half grand
in the life of a mortgage.
A free car!
And a pancreas systemically clean.

But, *panem sine circenses*, where's the kick?
Our three-score-plus tenure is a tease.
So, bring me wine and water, waiter, please.

Taking a Shine

The silver on the tap depreciates so soon,
hallmark of *the reliable plumber,*
who even forgot to send the bill,
popping it in, apologetically, a month in arrears,
the surface tarnish already underway.

A once-over with deep-scented, foaming Vamoose
and porcelain enamel gleams Ivanka bright,
against the faucet's further lustre loss.
Obligatory maidenhair fern spills
tasteful green across the tiles and grout.

Soft cloth and spray redeem the mirror
from dust and make-up scuffs and toothpaste specks,
unveil a Keatsian lover poised to kiss
your neck, caught perfectly in a freeze of time
admired Velazquez would appreciate.

Normal is a Travesty

song regretting prelapsarian times

There's nothing normal about normal.
Normal is looking kinda weird.
Ain't gonna be cosy and informal.
It's everything that you have ever feared.

Chorus
Normal is a travesty.   (x4, à la PIL *Anger is an energy*)

There's an embargo now on hugging.
Everyone keep six feet over there!
But the thing that's absolutely bugging
Is why that ******* Cummings is still here!

Johnson is testing, tracing, tracking,
Lying through his teeth to me and you.
See how the infrastructure's cracking.
Johnson hasn't got a ******* clue

We've been very good throughout the lockdown –
No eye tests . . . . . We didn't panic buy.
LOCKDOWN, LOCKDOWN, LOCKDOWN,
    LOCKDOWN, LOCKDOWN!
CLAP, CLAP, CLAP, CLAP, I don't wanna die!

9th July 2020

Boot Boy

The Universe ... the World ... Europe ...
the 'British' Isles ... the UK ... England ...
Hampshire ... Portsmouth ... PO1 2DD ...
The Isambard Kingdom Brunel boozer.

Isambard is a Norman name of Germanic origin: *'iron-bright'.*

It's Friday morning, it's half past ten.
We're in the presence of Wetherspoons supremo,
MR ... TIM ... MARTIN!
Gennlemen, raise your pints!

Tim reaches Pompey on the umpteenth leg
of his 100-pub crusade to prove that
a No-Deal Brexit is not really a 100-mile-an-hour
car crash (with the kids in the back).
Half a million beer mats can't be wrong, and yes, of course
we meant Jacob's Creek, not Châteauneuf-du-Pape.

Jacob was actually Bavarian, Tim. Sorry about that.

Our hero needs a haircut.
His bovver boots reflect a zealot's glint.

Matchwood Wetherspoons tabletops
won't withstand his thirteen stones,
so he plonks his plates of meat
astride two upholstered seats.

What in the name of Ruskin are you doing, Tim?
Which pallid ex-riveter
will catch toxocara canis
from what you've walked in on your hooves?

Bleeding in the B & B

Annie ran the B & B,
Chris, he had a shed.
Find her at Kilmore dot I E
(except in January: she's on the Med).

Chris, he took up carpentry,
chamfering away in his shed;
learnt tongue-and-groove and parquetry
from *The Woodworker's A to Z*.

Down in the snug at O'Connell's Bar
we were watching *Father Ted*.
That extra pint will do for you.
 I think that's what you said.

Stumbling out in the dead of night,
inching for the bathroom ahead ...
Glory be to Jesus! I'm bleeding
from a bloody great hole in my head.

Chris had fashioned a shelf for the kettle
on the wall by the side of the bed.
The construct and I had collided,
and I bled and I bled and I bled.

Now Annie she stints on black pudding.
Still and all – for the price – you're well fed.
But Chris, the dark horse that you'll never meet,
is the one will have you in the red.

Leaving Paris, Summer 2005

Send me a manuscript in duplicate.
This American in Paris is queering my pitch.
You can read in October if it's accepted.
But I leave Paris this week – my lease is up!

He preens under a Prévert beret, worn indoors,
black turtleneck – *de rigueur* –
pulled over his paunch and tucked
into what he would call slacks. Tight ass!
But he's the only show in town on Monday nights.

A lanky Slav cadaver, headlining,
purveys pain from Moldova or Lutsk,
her audience all costive deference.

Over pints at the break I commiserate
with a cheesed-off Dubliner in a linen suit.
This day and age … no fuckin' open mic!

We found our own *salon des refusés*
and swap recent work in an alcove.
I do *Est-ce qu'il est … ? till the Bloody Cows Come Home*
and give sympathetic ear to his
Elegy for a Broken Crack-pipe.

Est-ce qu'il est …?
till the Bloody Cows Come Home

Finalement.
Note that voiced '*e*' and how the suffix
'*ment*' denotes an adverb not a noun.

*Finalement, les Français n'ont pas à rougir
de leur niveau d'anglais.* (Métro, *première page*)

We read their *froideur* wrong, then: they were shy,
in-cer-tains of those Frenchless anglophones.
Peut-être.

But now *la langue véhiculaire* has got its wheels
and there's no stopping them.
Your timid '*deux qua-sawn, s'il vous plaît*'
is met by '*English? Bon!*'
Et voila! He's practising on you.
Your tentative engagement is derailed.
You've failed, my friend. You're
dis-qua-li-fi-é.

This will not do, this emulsion life,
in France but not of it,
more helpless than a babe in arms, for whom
the world will wait and cheer each syllable.
You can't bank on osmosis but you
won't truck with charlatans
who parcel out *la langue* in neat *clichés* –
Let's have a fun in French, one advert croons –
and *garantie par contrat* that you'll pass.

It's time you found
your modus operandi francophone.
High time you knew that knowing *le* from *la*
is *not* the finished article.
Read everything: *Le Monde, Libé, Métro,*
des publicités, des romans, des poèmes.
You're not a child buying ice cream at *piscines*
or booking surreal role-play *chambres libres -*
Est-ce qu'il est ... ? till the bloody cows come home.

Now, plunge inelegantly in.
(Franglais's okay.)
In time you'll learn to swim
in this pool *de langage étranger –*
not polite lengths with a polished stroke
but striking out with verve – *dans un lac ...*
une mer ... un ocean ... une lagune,
conversant with *les courants, les marées*
artistiques, sportives et politiques.
Sous le Pont Mirabeau tu vas faire un plouf d'extase!

Postcard

I don't know why but hello

whether to stay or to go

all things depending

hope never ending

I am elsewhere now, so

The Cretan Sonnets

(i) **Stubborn Resistance**

'There are some, I see, who say
we should not fight without superior,
or at least ample, air support.'
(Churchill to the House, and home to bed.)

'The necessary aircraft simply did not exist.'
Buckley, '52. Freyburg agreed.
Again, 'In Crete, for six months undisturbed,
defensive measures needed were not taken.'

Harried through Greece, in transit then in Crete,
Kiwis at Maleme were sacrificed
on Fortune's altar: sheer bleeding bad luck
saw them stuck.

As Junkers dropped their loads and Stukas dived
'stubborn resistance' was the counsel Churchill gave.

(ii) **Salute the Leaders**

November 1940, Brigadier
Tidbury forecast what would come in May.
In January, Gambier-Perry took the helm
for three weeks, prior to Egypt, after which
Lieutenant Colonel H. D Mather ran
the show pro tem till Feb 19.
Incoming Brigadier A. Galloway

commanded Creforce next, for a fortnight,
before Mather got the reins again and held
them this time until March 19.
'With no definite directive,' B.H. Chappell
did ten days' work till E. C. Weston came.
He lasted all of April until Wavell
delivered General Freyburg the black spot.

(iii) **Coming or Going**

On Souda Bay the ferryboats move out
to Athens and the scattered isles of Greece.
On westward slopes, descending to the bay,
lie graves of soldiers in a grove of peace.

The British on the left hold messages –
lines from Binyon or Sassoon.
Australians' in the centre are inscribed
with ranks, or badges of an infantry platoon.

The Kiwis to the right have plainer stones,
in circles carved *New Zealand* or the fern.
No messages, and often there's no name.
Known unto God is all you learn.

And everywhere such flowers as catch the heart
anele the souls doomed never to depart.

Lightning Source UK Ltd.
Milton Keynes UK
UKHW011604050521
383165UK00001B/69

9 781789 631968